MW00897971

WELCOME

GUEST NAME(S)

Scott & Susan House

DATES OF STAY: 12/11 - 12/13

TRAVELED FROM:

Spring Lake Farms
North Stafford, VA

MESSAGE TO THE HOST:

We're having such a wonderful stay. I just love the horseshoe pond. It's so nice to see the sun come up over the water + also set over the water as well. Saw a couple deer too! So cozy + peaceful ☺

FAVOURITE PLACES AND THINGS TO DO:

Absolutely Nothing! We fished a little + relaxed (we're from here)

GUEST NAME(S)

Ashley Parsley
Shaley Seger

DATES OF STAY: 2/20 - 2/21

TRAVELED FROM:

Culpeper, VA

MESSAGE TO THE HOST:

We had a really awesome girls night! It's so Peaceful here. We love the view and have already ~~already~~ talked about coming back in the Summer and fall!

FAVOURITE PLACES AND THINGS TO DO:

We didn't go anywhere but enjoyed the fire & smores! :)

GUEST NAME(S)

Jay + Kristin Mullins

DATES OF STAY: 3-5-2021 - 3-7-2021

TRAVELED FROM:

Perry Hall MD

MESSAGE TO THE HOST:

We had a great time here at horseshoe pond. I loved the house. We look forward to staying again

FAVOURITE PLACES AND THINGS TO DO:

We just relaxed all weekend at the house.

GUEST NAME(S)

Ryan, Jenn & Addison

DATES OF STAY: 3.12 - 3.14, 2021

TRAVELED FROM:

Gaithersburg, MD

MESSAGE TO THE HOST:

We had a fantastic time at Horseshoe Pond, the great hospitality from Tom & Denise made it easy to stay and relax all weekend. We look forward to staying again in the future. Thank you so much for everything!

FAVOURITE PLACES AND THINGS TO DO:

Stayed at Horseshoe Pond all weekend, went fishing and made smores by the fire

GUEST NAME(S)

_____

_____

DATES OF STAY:

TRAVELED FROM:

_____

_____

MESSAGE TO THE HOST:

_____

_____

_____

_____

_____

_____

_____

FAVOURITE PLACES AND THINGS TO DO:

_____

_____

GUEST NAME(S)

_____

_____

DATES OF STAY:

TRAVELED FROM:

_____

_____

MESSAGE TO THE HOST:

_____

_____

_____

_____

_____

_____

_____

FAVOURITE PLACES AND THINGS TO DO:

_____

_____

GUEST NAME(S)

_____

_____

DATES OF STAY:

TRAVELED FROM:

_____

_____

MESSAGE TO THE HOST:

_____

_____

_____

_____

_____

_____

_____

FAVOURITE PLACES AND THINGS TO DO:

_____

_____

_____

GUEST NAME(S)

_____

_____

DATES OF STAY:

TRAVELED FROM:

_____

_____

MESSAGE TO THE HOST:

_____

_____

_____

_____

_____

_____

_____

FAVOURITE PLACES AND THINGS TO DO:

_____

_____

GUEST NAME(S)

_____

_____

DATES OF STAY:

TRAVELED FROM:

_____

_____

MESSAGE TO THE HOST:

_____

_____

_____

_____

_____

_____

FAVOURITE PLACES AND THINGS TO DO:

_____

_____

GUEST NAME(S)

_____

_____

DATES OF STAY:

TRAVELED FROM:

_____

_____

MESSAGE TO THE HOST:

_____

_____

_____

_____

_____

_____

_____

FAVOURITE PLACES AND THINGS TO DO:

_____

_____

GUEST NAME(S)

_____

_____

DATES OF STAY:

TRAVELED FROM:

_____

_____

MESSAGE TO THE HOST:

_____

_____

_____

_____

_____

_____

_____

FAVOURITE PLACES AND THINGS TO DO:

_____

_____

GUEST NAME(S)

_____

_____

DATES OF STAY:

TRAVELED FROM:

_____

_____

MESSAGE TO THE HOST:

_____

_____

_____

_____

_____

_____

_____

FAVOURITE PLACES AND THINGS TO DO:

_____

_____

GUEST NAME(S)

_____

_____

DATES OF STAY:

TRAVELED FROM:

_____

_____

MESSAGE TO THE HOST:

_____

_____

_____

_____

_____

_____

FAVOURITE PLACES AND THINGS TO DO:

_____

_____

GUEST NAME(S)

_____

_____

DATES OF STAY:

TRAVELED FROM:

_____

_____

MESSAGE TO THE HOST:

_____

_____

_____

_____

_____

_____

_____

FAVOURITE PLACES AND THINGS TO DO:

_____

_____

GUEST NAME(S)

_____

_____

DATES OF STAY:

TRAVELED FROM:

_____

_____

MESSAGE TO THE HOST:

_____

_____

_____

_____

_____

_____

_____

FAVOURITE PLACES AND THINGS TO DO:

_____

_____

GUEST NAME(S)

_____

_____

DATES OF STAY:

TRAVELED FROM:

_____

_____

MESSAGE TO THE HOST:

_____

_____

_____

_____

_____

_____

_____

FAVOURITE PLACES AND THINGS TO DO:

_____

_____

GUEST NAME(S)

_____

_____

DATES OF STAY:

TRAVELED FROM:

_____

_____

MESSAGE TO THE HOST:

_____

_____

_____

_____

_____

_____

_____

FAVOURITE PLACES AND THINGS TO DO:

_____

_____

GUEST NAME(S)

_____

_____

DATES OF STAY:

TRAVELED FROM:

_____

_____

MESSAGE TO THE HOST:

_____

_____

_____

_____

_____

_____

_____

FAVOURITE PLACES AND THINGS TO DO:

_____

_____

_____

GUEST NAME(S)

_____

_____

DATES OF STAY:

TRAVELED FROM:

_____

_____

MESSAGE TO THE HOST:

_____

_____

_____

_____

_____

_____

_____

FAVOURITE PLACES AND THINGS TO DO:

_____

_____

GUEST NAME(S)

_____

_____

DATES OF STAY:

TRAVELED FROM:

_____

_____

MESSAGE TO THE HOST:

_____

_____

_____

_____

_____

_____

_____

FAVOURITE PLACES AND THINGS TO DO:

_____

_____

GUEST NAME(S)

_____

_____

DATES OF STAY:

TRAVELED FROM:

_____

_____

MESSAGE TO THE HOST:

_____

_____

_____

_____

_____

_____

_____

FAVOURITE PLACES AND THINGS TO DO:

_____

_____

GUEST NAME(S)

_____

_____

DATES OF STAY:

TRAVELED FROM:

_____

_____

MESSAGE TO THE HOST:

_____

_____

_____

_____

_____

_____

_____

FAVOURITE PLACES AND THINGS TO DO:

_____

_____

GUEST NAME(S)

_____

_____

DATES OF STAY:

TRAVELED FROM:

_____

_____

MESSAGE TO THE HOST:

_____

_____

_____

_____

_____

_____

_____

_____

FAVOURITE PLACES AND THINGS TO DO:

_____

_____

GUEST NAME(S)

_____

_____

DATES OF STAY:

TRAVELED FROM:

_____

_____

MESSAGE TO THE HOST:

_____

_____

_____

_____

_____

_____

_____

FAVOURITE PLACES AND THINGS TO DO:

_____

_____

GUEST NAME(S)

_____

_____

DATES OF STAY:

TRAVELED FROM:

_____

_____

MESSAGE TO THE HOST:

_____

_____

_____

_____

_____

_____

_____

FAVOURITE PLACES AND THINGS TO DO:

_____

_____

GUEST NAME(S)

_____

_____

MESSAGE TO THE HOST:

_____
_____
_____
_____
_____
_____
_____

DATES OF STAY:

TRAVELED FROM:

_____

_____

FAVOURITE PLACES AND THINGS TO DO:

_____
_____
_____

GUEST NAME(S)

_____

_____

DATES OF STAY:

TRAVELED FROM:

_____

_____

MESSAGE TO THE HOST:

_____

_____

_____

_____

_____

_____

_____

FAVOURITE PLACES AND THINGS TO DO:

_____

_____

GUEST NAME(S)

_____

_____

DATES OF STAY:

TRAVELED FROM:

_____

_____

MESSAGE TO THE HOST:

_____

_____

_____

_____

_____

_____

_____

FAVOURITE PLACES AND THINGS TO DO:

_____

_____

GUEST NAME(S)

_____

_____

DATES OF STAY:

TRAVELED FROM:

_____

_____

MESSAGE TO THE HOST:

_____

_____

_____

_____

_____

_____

_____

FAVOURITE PLACES AND THINGS TO DO:

_____

_____

GUEST NAME(S)

_____

_____

DATES OF STAY:

TRAVELED FROM:

_____

_____

MESSAGE TO THE HOST:

_____

_____

_____

_____

_____

_____

_____

FAVOURITE PLACES AND THINGS TO DO:

_____

_____

GUEST NAME(S)

_____

_____

DATES OF STAY:

TRAVELED FROM:

_____

_____

MESSAGE TO THE HOST:

_____

_____

_____

_____

_____

_____

_____

FAVOURITE PLACES AND THINGS TO DO:

_____

_____

GUEST NAME(S)

_____

_____

DATES OF STAY:

TRAVELED FROM:

_____

_____

MESSAGE TO THE HOST:

_____

_____

_____

_____

_____

_____

_____

FAVOURITE PLACES AND THINGS TO DO:

_____

_____

_____

GUEST NAME(S)

_____

_____

DATES OF STAY:

TRAVELED FROM:

_____

_____

MESSAGE TO THE HOST:

_____

_____

_____

_____

_____

_____

_____

FAVOURITE PLACES AND THINGS TO DO:

_____

_____

GUEST NAME(S)

_____

_____

DATES OF STAY:

TRAVELED FROM:

_____

_____

MESSAGE TO THE HOST:

_____

_____

_____

_____

_____

_____

_____

FAVOURITE PLACES AND THINGS TO DO:

_____

_____

_____

GUEST NAME(S)

_____

_____

DATES OF STAY:

TRAVELED FROM:

_____

_____

MESSAGE TO THE HOST:

_____

_____

_____

_____

_____

_____

_____

FAVOURITE PLACES AND THINGS TO DO:

_____

_____

GUEST NAME(S)

_____

_____

DATES OF STAY:

TRAVELED FROM:

_____

_____

MESSAGE TO THE HOST:

_____

_____

_____

_____

_____

_____

_____

FAVOURITE PLACES AND THINGS TO DO:

_____

_____

_____

GUEST NAME(S)

_____

_____

DATES OF STAY:

TRAVELED FROM:

_____

_____

MESSAGE TO THE HOST:

_____

_____

_____

_____

_____

_____

_____

_____

FAVOURITE PLACES AND THINGS TO DO:

_____

_____

GUEST NAME(S)

_____

_____

DATES OF STAY:

TRAVELED FROM:

_____

_____

MESSAGE TO THE HOST:

_____

_____

_____

_____

_____

_____

_____

FAVOURITE PLACES AND THINGS TO DO:

_____

_____

GUEST NAME(S)

_____

_____

DATES OF STAY:

TRAVELED FROM:

_____

_____

MESSAGE TO THE HOST:

_____

_____

_____

_____

_____

_____

_____

FAVOURITE PLACES AND THINGS TO DO:

_____

_____

GUEST NAME(S)

_____

_____

DATES OF STAY:

TRAVELED FROM:

_____

_____

MESSAGE TO THE HOST:

_____

_____

_____

_____

_____

_____

_____

FAVOURITE PLACES AND THINGS TO DO:

_____

_____

GUEST NAME(S)

_____

_____

DATES OF STAY:

TRAVELED FROM:

_____

_____

MESSAGE TO THE HOST:

_____

_____

_____

_____

_____

_____

_____

FAVOURITE PLACES AND THINGS TO DO:

_____

_____

GUEST NAME(S)

_____

_____

DATES OF STAY:

TRAVELED FROM:

_____

_____

MESSAGE TO THE HOST:

_____

_____

_____

_____

_____

_____

_____

FAVOURITE PLACES AND THINGS TO DO:

_____

_____

GUEST NAME(S)

_____

_____

DATES OF STAY:

TRAVELED FROM:

_____

_____

MESSAGE TO THE HOST:

_____

_____

_____

_____

_____

_____

_____

FAVOURITE PLACES AND THINGS TO DO:

_____

_____

GUEST NAME(S)

_____

_____

DATES OF STAY:

TRAVELED FROM:

_____

_____

MESSAGE TO THE HOST:

_____

_____

_____

_____

_____

_____

_____

_____

FAVOURITE PLACES AND THINGS TO DO:

_____

_____

_____

GUEST NAME(S)

_____

_____

DATES OF STAY:

TRAVELED FROM:

_____

_____

MESSAGE TO THE HOST:

_____

_____

_____

_____

_____

_____

_____

FAVOURITE PLACES AND THINGS TO DO:

_____

_____

GUEST NAME(S)

_____

_____

DATES OF STAY:

TRAVELED FROM:

_____

_____

MESSAGE TO THE HOST:

_____

_____

_____

_____

_____

_____

_____

FAVOURITE PLACES AND THINGS TO DO:

_____

_____

_____

GUEST NAME(S)

_____

_____

DATES OF STAY:

TRAVELED FROM:

_____

_____

MESSAGE TO THE HOST:

_____

_____

_____

_____

_____

_____

FAVOURITE PLACES AND THINGS TO DO:

_____

_____

GUEST NAME(S)

_____

_____

DATES OF STAY:

TRAVELED FROM:

_____

_____

MESSAGE TO THE HOST:

_____

_____

_____

_____

_____

_____

_____

FAVOURITE PLACES AND THINGS TO DO:

_____

_____

GUEST NAME(S)

_____

_____

DATES OF STAY:

TRAVELED FROM:

_____

_____

MESSAGE TO THE HOST:

_____

_____

_____

_____

_____

_____

_____

FAVOURITE PLACES AND THINGS TO DO:

_____

_____

GUEST NAME(S)

_____

_____

DATES OF STAY:

TRAVELED FROM:

_____

_____

MESSAGE TO THE HOST:

_____

_____

_____

_____

_____

_____

_____

FAVOURITE PLACES AND THINGS TO DO:

_____

_____

GUEST NAME(S)

_____

_____

DATES OF STAY:

TRAVELED FROM:

_____

_____

MESSAGE TO THE HOST:

_____

_____

_____

_____

_____

_____

_____

FAVOURITE PLACES AND THINGS TO DO:

_____

_____

GUEST NAME(S)

_____

_____

DATES OF STAY:

TRAVELED FROM:

_____

_____

MESSAGE TO THE HOST:

_____

_____

_____

_____

_____

_____

_____

FAVOURITE PLACES AND THINGS TO DO:

_____

_____

GUEST NAME(S)

_____

_____

DATES OF STAY:

TRAVELED FROM:

_____

_____

MESSAGE TO THE HOST:

_____

_____

_____

_____

_____

_____

_____

FAVOURITE PLACES AND THINGS TO DO:

_____

_____

GUEST NAME(S)

_____

_____

DATES OF STAY:

TRAVELED FROM:

_____

_____

MESSAGE TO THE HOST:

_____

_____

_____

_____

_____

_____

_____

FAVOURITE PLACES AND THINGS TO DO:

_____

_____

GUEST NAME(S)

_____

_____

DATES OF STAY:

TRAVELED FROM:

_____

_____

MESSAGE TO THE HOST:

_____

_____

_____

_____

_____

_____

_____

FAVOURITE PLACES AND THINGS TO DO:

_____

_____

GUEST NAME(S)

_____

_____

DATES OF STAY:

TRAVELED FROM:

_____

_____

MESSAGE TO THE HOST:

_____

_____

_____

_____

_____

_____

_____

FAVOURITE PLACES AND THINGS TO DO:

_____

_____

GUEST NAME(S)

_____

_____

DATES OF STAY:

TRAVELED FROM:

_____

_____

MESSAGE TO THE HOST:

_____

_____

_____

_____

_____

_____

_____

FAVOURITE PLACES AND THINGS TO DO:

_____

_____

GUEST NAME(S)

_____

_____

DATES OF STAY:

TRAVELED FROM:

_____

_____

MESSAGE TO THE HOST:

_____

_____

_____

_____

_____

_____

FAVOURITE PLACES AND THINGS TO DO:

_____

_____

GUEST NAME(S)

_____

_____

DATES OF STAY:

TRAVELED FROM:

_____

_____

MESSAGE TO THE HOST:

_____

_____

_____

_____

_____

_____

_____

FAVOURITE PLACES AND THINGS TO DO:

_____

_____

_____

GUEST NAME(S)

_____

_____

DATES OF STAY:

TRAVELED FROM:

_____

_____

MESSAGE TO THE HOST:

_____

_____

_____

_____

_____

_____

_____

FAVOURITE PLACES AND THINGS TO DO:

_____

_____

GUEST NAME(S)

_____

_____

DATES OF STAY:

TRAVELED FROM:

_____

_____

MESSAGE TO THE HOST:

_____

_____

_____

_____

_____

_____

_____

FAVOURITE PLACES AND THINGS TO DO:

_____

_____

GUEST NAME(S)

_____

_____

MESSAGE TO THE HOST:

_____

_____

_____

_____

_____

_____

DATES OF STAY:

TRAVELED FROM:

_____

_____

FAVOURITE PLACES AND THINGS TO DO:

_____

_____

GUEST NAME(S)

_____

_____

DATES OF STAY:

TRAVELED FROM:

_____

_____

MESSAGE TO THE HOST:

_____

_____

_____

_____

_____

_____

_____

FAVOURITE PLACES AND THINGS TO DO:

_____

_____

GUEST NAME(S)

_____

_____

DATES OF STAY:

TRAVELED FROM:

_____

_____

MESSAGE TO THE HOST:

_____

_____

_____

_____

_____

_____

_____

FAVOURITE PLACES AND THINGS TO DO:

_____

_____

GUEST NAME(S)

_____

_____

DATES OF STAY:

TRAVELED FROM:

_____

_____

MESSAGE TO THE HOST:

_____

_____

_____

_____

_____

_____

_____

_____

FAVOURITE PLACES AND THINGS TO DO:

_____

_____

GUEST NAME(S)

DATES OF STAY:

TRAVELED FROM:

MESSAGE TO THE HOST:

FAVOURITE PLACES AND THINGS TO DO:

GUEST NAME(S)

_____

_____

DATES OF STAY:

TRAVELED FROM:

_____

_____

MESSAGE TO THE HOST:

_____

_____

_____

_____

_____

_____

_____

FAVOURITE PLACES AND THINGS TO DO:

_____

_____

GUEST NAME(S)

_____

_____

DATES OF STAY:

TRAVELED FROM:

_____

_____

MESSAGE TO THE HOST:

_____

_____

_____

_____

_____

_____

_____

FAVOURITE PLACES AND THINGS TO DO:

_____

_____

GUEST NAME(S)

_____

_____

DATES OF STAY:

TRAVELED FROM:

_____

_____

MESSAGE TO THE HOST:

_____

_____

_____

_____

_____

_____

FAVOURITE PLACES AND THINGS TO DO:

_____

_____

GUEST NAME(S)

_____

_____

DATES OF STAY:

TRAVELED FROM:

_____

_____

MESSAGE TO THE HOST:

_____

_____

_____

_____

_____

_____

_____

FAVOURITE PLACES AND THINGS TO DO:

_____

_____

_____

GUEST NAME(S)

_____

_____

DATES OF STAY:

TRAVELED FROM:

_____

_____

MESSAGE TO THE HOST:

_____

_____

_____

_____

_____

_____

_____

FAVOURITE PLACES AND THINGS TO DO:

_____

_____

GUEST NAME(S)

_____

_____

DATES OF STAY:

TRAVELED FROM:

_____

_____

MESSAGE TO THE HOST:

_____

_____

_____

_____

_____

_____

_____

FAVOURITE PLACES AND THINGS TO DO:

_____

_____

GUEST NAME(S)

_____

_____

DATES OF STAY:

TRAVELED FROM:

_____

_____

MESSAGE TO THE HOST:

_____

_____

_____

_____

_____

_____

_____

FAVOURITE PLACES AND THINGS TO DO:

_____

_____

GUEST NAME(S)

_____

_____

DATES OF STAY:

TRAVELED FROM:

_____

_____

MESSAGE TO THE HOST:

_____

_____

_____

_____

_____

_____

_____

FAVOURITE PLACES AND THINGS TO DO:

_____

_____

_____

GUEST NAME(S)

_____

_____

DATES OF STAY:

TRAVELED FROM:

_____

_____

MESSAGE TO THE HOST:

_____

_____

_____

_____

_____

_____

_____

FAVOURITE PLACES AND THINGS TO DO:

_____

_____

GUEST NAME(S)

_____

_____

DATES OF STAY:

TRAVELED FROM:

_____

_____

MESSAGE TO THE HOST:

_____

_____

_____

_____

_____

_____

_____

FAVOURITE PLACES AND THINGS TO DO:

_____

_____

_____

GUEST NAME(S)

_____

_____

DATES OF STAY:

TRAVELED FROM:

_____

_____

MESSAGE TO THE HOST:

_____

_____

_____

_____

_____

_____

_____

FAVOURITE PLACES AND THINGS TO DO:

_____

_____

GUEST NAME(S)

_____

_____

DATES OF STAY:

TRAVELED FROM:

_____

_____

MESSAGE TO THE HOST:

_____

_____

_____

_____

_____

_____

_____

FAVOURITE PLACES AND THINGS TO DO:

_____

_____

GUEST NAME(S)

_____

_____

DATES OF STAY:

TRAVELED FROM:

_____

_____

MESSAGE TO THE HOST:

_____

_____

_____

_____

_____

_____

_____

FAVOURITE PLACES AND THINGS TO DO:

_____

_____

GUEST NAME(S)

_____

_____

DATES OF STAY:

TRAVELED FROM:

_____

_____

MESSAGE TO THE HOST:

_____

_____

_____

_____

_____

_____

_____

FAVOURITE PLACES AND THINGS TO DO:

_____

_____

GUEST NAME(S)

_____

_____

DATES OF STAY:

TRAVELED FROM:

_____

_____

MESSAGE TO THE HOST:

_____

_____

_____

_____

_____

_____

_____

FAVOURITE PLACES AND THINGS TO DO:

_____

_____

GUEST NAME(S)

_____

_____

DATES OF STAY:

TRAVELED FROM:

_____

_____

MESSAGE TO THE HOST:

_____

_____

_____

_____

_____

_____

_____

FAVOURITE PLACES AND THINGS TO DO:

_____

_____

GUEST NAME(S)

_____

_____

DATES OF STAY:

TRAVELED FROM:

_____

_____

MESSAGE TO THE HOST:

_____

_____

_____

_____

_____

_____

_____

FAVOURITE PLACES AND THINGS TO DO:

_____

_____

GUEST NAME(S)

_____

_____

DATES OF STAY:

TRAVELED FROM:

_____

_____

MESSAGE TO THE HOST:

_____

_____

_____

_____

_____

_____

_____

_____

FAVOURITE PLACES AND THINGS TO DO:

_____

_____

GUEST NAME(S)

_____

_____

DATES OF STAY:

TRAVELED FROM:

_____

_____

MESSAGE TO THE HOST:

_____

_____

_____

_____

_____

_____

_____

_____

FAVOURITE PLACES AND THINGS TO DO:

_____

_____

GUEST NAME(S)

_____

_____

DATES OF STAY:

TRAVELED FROM:

_____

_____

MESSAGE TO THE HOST:

_____

_____

_____

_____

_____

_____

_____

FAVOURITE PLACES AND THINGS TO DO:

_____

_____

GUEST NAME(S)

_____

_____

DATES OF STAY:

TRAVELED FROM:

_____

_____

MESSAGE TO THE HOST:

_____

_____

_____

_____

_____

_____

_____

FAVOURITE PLACES AND THINGS TO DO:

_____

_____

GUEST NAME(S)

_____

_____

DATES OF STAY:

TRAVELED FROM:

_____

_____

MESSAGE TO THE HOST:

_____

_____

_____

_____

_____

_____

_____

FAVOURITE PLACES AND THINGS TO DO:

_____

_____

GUEST NAME(S)

_____

_____

DATES OF STAY:

TRAVELED FROM:

_____

_____

MESSAGE TO THE HOST:

_____

_____

_____

_____

_____

_____

_____

FAVOURITE PLACES AND THINGS TO DO:

_____

_____

GUEST NAME(S)

_____

_____

DATES OF STAY:

TRAVELED FROM:

_____

_____

MESSAGE TO THE HOST:

_____

_____

_____

_____

_____

_____

_____

FAVOURITE PLACES AND THINGS TO DO:

_____

_____

_____

GUEST NAME(S)

_____

_____

DATES OF STAY:

TRAVELED FROM:

_____

_____

MESSAGE TO THE HOST:

_____

_____

_____

_____

_____

_____

_____

FAVOURITE PLACES AND THINGS TO DO:

_____

_____

GUEST NAME(S)

_____

_____

DATES OF STAY:

TRAVELED FROM:

_____

_____

MESSAGE TO THE HOST:

_____

_____

_____

_____

_____

_____

_____

FAVOURITE PLACES AND THINGS TO DO:

_____

_____

GUEST NAME(S)

_____

_____

DATES OF STAY:

TRAVELED FROM:

_____

_____

MESSAGE TO THE HOST:

_____

_____

_____

_____

_____

_____

_____

FAVOURITE PLACES AND THINGS TO DO:

_____

_____

GUEST NAME(S)

_____

_____

DATES OF STAY:

TRAVELED FROM:

_____

_____

MESSAGE TO THE HOST:

_____

_____

_____

_____

_____

_____

_____

FAVOURITE PLACES AND THINGS TO DO:

_____

_____

GUEST NAME(S)

_____

_____

DATES OF STAY:

TRAVELED FROM:

_____

_____

MESSAGE TO THE HOST:

_____

_____

_____

_____

_____

_____

_____

FAVOURITE PLACES AND THINGS TO DO:

_____

_____

GUEST NAME(S)

_____

_____

DATES OF STAY:

TRAVELED FROM:

_____

_____

MESSAGE TO THE HOST:

_____

_____

_____

_____

_____

_____

_____

FAVOURITE PLACES AND THINGS TO DO:

_____

_____

GUEST NAME(S)

_____

_____

DATES OF STAY:

TRAVELED FROM:

_____

_____

MESSAGE TO THE HOST:

_____

_____

_____

_____

_____

_____

_____

_____

FAVOURITE PLACES AND THINGS TO DO:

_____

_____

GUEST NAME(S)

_____

_____

DATES OF STAY:

TRAVELED FROM:

_____

_____

MESSAGE TO THE HOST:

_____

_____

_____

_____

_____

_____

_____

FAVOURITE PLACES AND THINGS TO DO:

_____

_____

GUEST NAME(S)

_____

_____

DATES OF STAY:

TRAVELED FROM:

_____

_____

MESSAGE TO THE HOST:

_____

_____

_____

_____

_____

_____

_____

FAVOURITE PLACES AND THINGS TO DO:

_____

_____

GUEST NAME(S)

_____

_____

DATES OF STAY:

TRAVELED FROM:

_____

_____

MESSAGE TO THE HOST:

_____

_____

_____

_____

_____

_____

_____

FAVOURITE PLACES AND THINGS TO DO:

_____

_____

GUEST NAME(S)

_____

_____

DATES OF STAY:

TRAVELED FROM:

_____

_____

MESSAGE TO THE HOST:

_____

_____

_____

_____

_____

_____

_____

FAVOURITE PLACES AND THINGS TO DO:

_____

_____

GUEST NAME(S)

_____

_____

DATES OF STAY:

TRAVELED FROM:

_____

_____

MESSAGE TO THE HOST:

_____

_____

_____

_____

_____

_____

_____

FAVOURITE PLACES AND THINGS TO DO:

_____

_____

GUEST NAME(S)

_____

_____

DATES OF STAY:

TRAVELED FROM:

_____

_____

MESSAGE TO THE HOST:

_____

_____

_____

_____

_____

_____

_____

FAVOURITE PLACES AND THINGS TO DO:

_____

_____

GUEST NAME(S)

_____

_____

DATES OF STAY:

TRAVELED FROM:

_____

_____

MESSAGE TO THE HOST:

_____

_____

_____

_____

_____

_____

_____

FAVOURITE PLACES AND THINGS TO DO:

_____

_____

GUEST NAME(S)

_____

_____

DATES OF STAY:

TRAVELED FROM:

_____

_____

MESSAGE TO THE HOST:

_____

_____

_____

_____

_____

_____

_____

FAVOURITE PLACES AND THINGS TO DO:

_____

_____

GUEST NAME(S)

_____

_____

DATES OF STAY:

TRAVELED FROM:

_____

_____

MESSAGE TO THE HOST:

_____

_____

_____

_____

_____

_____

_____

FAVOURITE PLACES AND THINGS TO DO:

_____

_____

GUEST NAME(S)

_____

_____

DATES OF STAY:

TRAVELED FROM:

_____

_____

MESSAGE TO THE HOST:

_____

_____

_____

_____

_____

_____

_____

FAVOURITE PLACES AND THINGS TO DO:

_____

_____

GUEST NAME(S)

_____

_____

DATES OF STAY:

TRAVELED FROM:

_____

_____

MESSAGE TO THE HOST:

_____

_____

_____

_____

_____

_____

_____

FAVOURITE PLACES AND THINGS TO DO:

_____

_____

GUEST NAME(S)

_____

_____

DATES OF STAY:

TRAVELED FROM:

_____

_____

MESSAGE TO THE HOST:

_____

_____

_____

_____

_____

_____

_____

_____

FAVOURITE PLACES AND THINGS TO DO:

_____

_____

GUEST NAME(S)

_____

_____

DATES OF STAY:

TRAVELED FROM:

_____

_____

MESSAGE TO THE HOST:

_____

_____

_____

_____

_____

_____

_____

_____

FAVOURITE PLACES AND THINGS TO DO:

_____

_____

_____

GUEST NAME(S)

_____

_____

DATES OF STAY:

TRAVELED FROM:

_____

_____

MESSAGE TO THE HOST:

_____

_____

_____

_____

_____

_____

_____

FAVOURITE PLACES AND THINGS TO DO:

_____

_____

GUEST NAME(S)

_____

_____

DATES OF STAY:

TRAVELED FROM:

_____

_____

MESSAGE TO THE HOST:

_____

_____

_____

_____

_____

_____

_____

FAVOURITE PLACES AND THINGS TO DO:

_____

_____

GUEST NAME(S)

_____

_____

DATES OF STAY:

TRAVELED FROM:

_____

_____

MESSAGE TO THE HOST:

_____

_____

_____

_____

_____

_____

_____

FAVOURITE PLACES AND THINGS TO DO:

_____

_____

GUEST NAME(S)

_____

_____

DATES OF STAY:

TRAVELED FROM:

_____

_____

MESSAGE TO THE HOST:

_____

_____

_____

_____

_____

_____

FAVOURITE PLACES AND THINGS TO DO:

_____

_____

GUEST NAME(S)

_____

_____

DATES OF STAY:

TRAVELED FROM:

_____

_____

MESSAGE TO THE HOST:

_____

_____

_____

_____

_____

_____

_____

FAVOURITE PLACES AND THINGS TO DO:

_____

_____

GUEST NAME(S)

_____

_____

DATES OF STAY:

TRAVELED FROM:

_____

_____

MESSAGE TO THE HOST:

_____

_____

_____

_____

_____

_____

_____

FAVOURITE PLACES AND THINGS TO DO:

_____

_____

GUEST NAME(S)

_____

_____

DATES OF STAY:

TRAVELED FROM:

_____

_____

MESSAGE TO THE HOST:

_____

_____

_____

_____

_____

_____

_____

FAVOURITE PLACES AND THINGS TO DO:

_____

_____

GUEST NAME(S)

_____

_____

DATES OF STAY:

TRAVELED FROM:

_____

_____

MESSAGE TO THE HOST:

_____

_____

_____

_____

_____

_____

_____

_____

FAVOURITE PLACES AND THINGS TO DO:

_____

_____

GUEST NAME(S)

_____

_____

DATES OF STAY:

TRAVELED FROM:

MESSAGE TO THE HOST:

_____

_____

_____

_____

_____

_____

_____

FAVOURITE PLACES AND THINGS TO DO:

_____

_____

GUEST NAME(S)

_____

_____

DATES OF STAY:

TRAVELED FROM:

_____

_____

MESSAGE TO THE HOST:

_____

_____

_____

_____

_____

_____

_____

_____

FAVOURITE PLACES AND THINGS TO DO:

_____

_____

_____

GUEST NAME(S)

_____

_____

DATES OF STAY:

TRAVELED FROM:

_____

_____

MESSAGE TO THE HOST:

_____

_____

_____

_____

_____

_____

FAVOURITE PLACES AND THINGS TO DO:

_____

_____

GUEST NAME(S)

_____

_____

DATES OF STAY:

TRAVELED FROM:

_____

_____

MESSAGE TO THE HOST:

_____

_____

_____

_____

_____

_____

_____

FAVOURITE PLACES AND THINGS TO DO:

_____

_____

GUEST NAME(S)

_____

_____

DATES OF STAY:

TRAVELED FROM:

_____

_____

MESSAGE TO THE HOST:

_____

_____

_____

_____

_____

_____

_____

FAVOURITE PLACES AND THINGS TO DO:

_____

_____

GUEST NAME(S)

_____

_____

DATES OF STAY:

TRAVELED FROM:

_____

_____

MESSAGE TO THE HOST:

_____

_____

_____

_____

_____

_____

_____

FAVOURITE PLACES AND THINGS TO DO:

_____

_____

GUEST NAME(S)

_____

_____

DATES OF STAY:

TRAVELED FROM:

_____

_____

MESSAGE TO THE HOST:

_____

_____

_____

_____

_____

_____

_____

FAVOURITE PLACES AND THINGS TO DO:

_____

_____

GUEST NAME(S)

_____

_____

DATES OF STAY:

TRAVELED FROM:

_____

_____

MESSAGE TO THE HOST:

_____

_____

_____

_____

_____

_____

_____

_____

FAVOURITE PLACES AND THINGS TO DO:

_____

_____

GUEST NAME(S)

_____

_____

DATES OF STAY:

TRAVELED FROM:

_____

_____

MESSAGE TO THE HOST:

_____

_____

_____

_____

_____

_____

_____

FAVOURITE PLACES AND THINGS TO DO:

_____

_____

GUEST NAME(S)

_____

_____

DATES OF STAY:

TRAVELED FROM:

_____

_____

MESSAGE TO THE HOST:

_____

_____

_____

_____

_____

_____

_____

FAVOURITE PLACES AND THINGS TO DO:

_____

_____

GUEST NAME(S)

_____

_____

DATES OF STAY:

TRAVELED FROM:

_____

_____

MESSAGE TO THE HOST:

_____

_____

_____

_____

_____

_____

_____

FAVOURITE PLACES AND THINGS TO DO:

_____

_____

GUEST NAME(S)

_____

_____

DATES OF STAY:

TRAVELED FROM:

_____

_____

MESSAGE TO THE HOST:

_____

_____

_____

_____

_____

_____

_____

FAVOURITE PLACES AND THINGS TO DO:

_____

_____

GUEST NAME(S)

_____

_____

DATES OF STAY:

TRAVELED FROM:

_____

_____

MESSAGE TO THE HOST:

_____

_____

_____

_____

_____

_____

_____

FAVOURITE PLACES AND THINGS TO DO:

_____

_____

GUEST NAME(S)

_____

_____

DATES OF STAY:

TRAVELED FROM:

_____

_____

MESSAGE TO THE HOST:

_____

_____

_____

_____

_____

_____

_____

FAVOURITE PLACES AND THINGS TO DO:

_____

_____

GUEST NAME(S)

_____

_____

DATES OF STAY:

TRAVELED FROM:

_____

_____

MESSAGE TO THE HOST:

_____

_____

_____

_____

_____

_____

_____

FAVOURITE PLACES AND THINGS TO DO:

_____

_____

GUEST NAME(S)

_____

_____

DATES OF STAY:

TRAVELED FROM:

_____

_____

MESSAGE TO THE HOST:

_____

_____

_____

_____

_____

_____

_____

FAVOURITE PLACES AND THINGS TO DO:

_____

_____

GUEST NAME(S)

_____

_____

DATES OF STAY:

TRAVELED FROM:

_____

_____

MESSAGE TO THE HOST:

_____

_____

_____

_____

_____

_____

_____

FAVOURITE PLACES AND THINGS TO DO:

_____

_____

GUEST NAME(S)

_____

_____

DATES OF STAY:

TRAVELED FROM:

_____

_____

MESSAGE TO THE HOST:

_____

_____

_____

_____

_____

_____

_____

FAVOURITE PLACES AND THINGS TO DO:

_____

_____

GUEST NAME(S)

_____

_____

DATES OF STAY:

TRAVELED FROM:

_____

_____

MESSAGE TO THE HOST:

_____

_____

_____

_____

_____

_____

_____

FAVOURITE PLACES AND THINGS TO DO:

_____

_____

GUEST NAME(S)

_____

_____

DATES OF STAY:

TRAVELED FROM:

_____

_____

MESSAGE TO THE HOST:

_____

_____

_____

_____

_____

_____

_____

FAVOURITE PLACES AND THINGS TO DO:

_____

_____

GUEST NAME(S)

_____

_____

DATES OF STAY:

TRAVELED FROM:

_____

_____

MESSAGE TO THE HOST:

_____

_____

_____

_____

_____

_____

_____

FAVOURITE PLACES AND THINGS TO DO:

_____

_____

GUEST NAME(S)

_____

_____

DATES OF STAY:

TRAVELED FROM:

_____

_____

MESSAGE TO THE HOST:

_____

_____

_____

_____

_____

_____

_____

FAVOURITE PLACES AND THINGS TO DO:

_____

_____

GUEST NAME(S)

_____

_____

DATES OF STAY:

TRAVELED FROM:

_____

_____

MESSAGE TO THE HOST:

_____

_____

_____

_____

_____

_____

FAVOURITE PLACES AND THINGS TO DO:

_____

_____

GUEST NAME(S)

_____

_____

DATES OF STAY:

TRAVELED FROM:

_____

_____

MESSAGE TO THE HOST:

_____

_____

_____

_____

_____

_____

_____

_____

FAVOURITE PLACES AND THINGS TO DO:

_____

_____

GUEST NAME(S)

_____

_____

DATES OF STAY:

TRAVELED FROM:

_____

_____

MESSAGE TO THE HOST:

_____

_____

_____

_____

_____

_____

_____

_____

FAVOURITE PLACES AND THINGS TO DO:

_____

_____

GUEST NAME(S)

_____

_____

DATES OF STAY:

TRAVELED FROM:

_____

_____

MESSAGE TO THE HOST:

_____

_____

_____

_____

_____

_____

_____

_____

FAVOURITE PLACES AND THINGS TO DO:

_____

_____

_____

GUEST NAME(S)

_____

_____

DATES OF STAY:

TRAVELED FROM:

_____

_____

MESSAGE TO THE HOST:

_____

_____

_____

_____

_____

_____

FAVOURITE PLACES AND THINGS TO DO:

_____

_____

GUEST NAME(S)

_____

_____

DATES OF STAY:

TRAVELED FROM:

_____

_____

MESSAGE TO THE HOST:

_____

_____

_____

_____

_____

_____

_____

FAVOURITE PLACES AND THINGS TO DO:

_____

_____

GUEST NAME(S)

_____

_____

DATES OF STAY:

TRAVELED FROM:

_____

_____

MESSAGE TO THE HOST:

_____

_____

_____

_____

_____

_____

_____

FAVOURITE PLACES AND THINGS TO DO:

_____

_____

GUEST NAME(S)

_____

_____

DATES OF STAY:

TRAVELED FROM:

_____

_____

MESSAGE TO THE HOST:

_____

_____

_____

_____

_____

_____

_____

FAVOURITE PLACES AND THINGS TO DO:

_____

_____

GUEST NAME(S)

_____

_____

DATES OF STAY:

TRAVELED FROM:

_____

_____

MESSAGE TO THE HOST:

_____

_____

_____

_____

_____

_____

FAVOURITE PLACES AND THINGS TO DO:

_____

_____